GOIN

Anthony Thwaite

GOING OUT

ENITHARMON PRESS

First published in 2015
by Enitharmon Press
10 Bury Place
London WC1A 2JL

www.enitharmon.co.uk

Distributed in the UK by
Central Books
99 Wallis Road
London E9 5LN

Distributed in the USA and Canada by
Independent Publishers Group
814 North Franklin Street
Chicago, IL 60610
USA
www.ipgbook.com

ISBN: 978-1-910392-00-3

Enitharmon Press gratefully acknowledges the financial support of
Arts Council England, through Grants for the Arts.

British Library Cataloguing-in-Publication Data.
A catalogue record for this book is available
from the British Library.

Designed in Albertina by Libanus Press
and printed in England by
Short Run Press

CONTENTS

for Ann,
who gave me the title

GOING OUT

Light bulbs, parties, jaunts, the final things –
The last most thought about at eighty-four,
Now as I gingerly change one of the first.
As for the second and third, not much these days,
Lacking an appetite for either. Drink –
A pale dilution, watered wine; no taste
For bad behaviour, mad hilarity,
Or staying up too late.
                              Or fashions, either –
I never paid attention to such things,
Not noticing when skirts went up or down,
Or poets began each line with lower case.

Last orders, ending up, or final things –
All titles with a flavour of last words,
All leading up to this one: going out.

THE ARK AMONG THE FLAGS

All the abandoned, never found or claimed;
The long-lost, nameless, scorned, or blackly named;
The scapegoats, stoned and cast away and blamed

For nothing but their prayer-words or their skin,
For being nothing but what they had always been,
Made nothing because of some lost origin –

Picked up today in Exodus, and read
Aloud again here, while centuries of dead
Hear silently what goes on being done, and said.

Under those eaves
In Borrage Lane,
Taking his leave
Snatched for a few hours,
Trying to catch the true tone
Of what he had known
And would go back to soon,
Above all Above all
Not concerned, scratched out, restored,
Each considered word
Above all, I am not concerned
With Poetry
And the blossom like confetti
The Poetry is in the pity.

TONGUES

So many words, fragments of language, sounds
Fractured, diffused, shifted, made obsolete,
Suppressed, remoulded, or sent underground,
Hieratic gestures, chatter in the street –

And here assembled, once, early that day
When many came, the squandered and the lost,
With broken words and whole, to rave and pray,
And Babel reconciled in Pentecost.

THE WALKING MAD

The streets of London are full of the walking mad,
Muttering, snarling, angrily answering
Someone who's never there.
Sometimes you catch a ferocious, direct stare
By chance, unaware of anything,
A furnace's blind glare.

Where have they come from, where are they going,
What is the matter, why have they come to this?
They crackle and spit, they fume
In the bright morning, and in the gathering gloom
They pour their grim energies
Into a stifled room.

They cannot get out, they are trapped in fire,
They are primed to explode, they spin
A Catherine wheel that's lit
By a long sputtering fuse, and it
Lets no one out or in.
Their rage immoderate,

They cannot see themselves but travel blind
Hurling obscenities at all around,
Hurrying on to spray
Another street with accusations. They
Are obdurate, iron-bound,
And do not go away.

HISTORY LESSON

The king went into exile. Little blood was shed.
Peace came and smiled at us. New schools were built.
Thanks were extended, fervent prayers were said.
No one throughout the land felt any guilt,
For none had sinned.
                 And soon there came the day
They told us it was *we* should make the laws,
New promulgations, pristine ways to say
This was the truth, that was the wicked cause.

And then the righteous stood in judgement, doors
Opened and closed to keep the prisoners in.
Gallows went up, the true-in-heart's just cause
Wiped out the whole mistaken opposition.

And so the land was cleansed as blood was shed.
Our leader smiled at us. Prisons were built
Across the desert while our prayers were said.
No one throughout the land felt any guilt

For all the sinful were in jail, or dead.

ANNUNCIATION

Why was he here
Filling the room
With light, and fear
Filling her womb?
What was he saying
Under his wings
As she was praying?
Impossible things:
Promise of birth,
God as the father,
Heaven and earth
In human feature …
What could she say
But bow her head
As he went away
With so much not said.

'My soul doth magnify …'
She whispered there,
'The Lord have mercy'
In the bright air.

MEMORIES

Fresh as rain, far off and sad,
The memories of what we had
And where we had them, long ago –
To bring them back, all sparkling new
Like something to look forward to
Spills helplessly, as to and fro
The scattered remnants come and go:

As when I play this music, night after night,
And when the wretched thing sticks with a mad howl
At the same place, as it always does –
First shriek, then buzz,
Then muffled growl,
And memories lose ground,
And sound, and sense, and sight.

NIGHT THOUGHTS REVISITED

Speaking as best I may, or as I might
If the day failed and all there was was night,
I look for something which could still be light.

All round are shadows, hints at shapes of things,
Glints of what was illumination, wings
Brushing my face with unseen featherings.

The words stick in my throat and make me choke,
Thick with impediment, a pall of smoke
Over the crushed pillow when I woke.

Come to me, then. Comfort me as I stay
A moment longer, looking for a way
To lead me to the promise of the day.

AT ORFORD NESS

Across these acres of degraded shingle
In process of continual ruination
There flies a gull, a single
Pulse of free life above
Remnants of mutually assured destruction.
Steadily beyond, the waves move.

ACCISMUS

When we speak
We mean more than we say.
Words do not go away.
Whatever dumb compulsions urge us on
We are too weak
To damp them down.
Accismus is our way:
'A feigned refusal of what is most desired.'
The will is tired,
Gives in too easily, lies there
Pretending not to care
Whatever's thrown away and burned,
And nothing left except this smoky air
As if it happened when my back was turned.

LIBYA

Thick sand, the ghibli blowing hard,
And the flickering screen bangs back the remembered place
Now loud with shots and shouts and running men,
And I remember when
We fled that place, and felt the smell of fear,
And heard the thud of guns and saw the fire
Eat up Bedussa's timber-yard,
And the collapsed look on Saad's face
When we came down the stairs
At 3 a.m. and caught the convoy out,
And all about
The smoke and panic, nothing certain, till
It all comes round again
But it is now, not then:
Nineteen sixty-seven
Shrinks to this flickering screen,
Is now, and loud with shots and running men,
And shouts, and thick sand blowing,
The ghibli blowing hard.

LUSTRATION

After the day's dig, I wash my hands.

Under the tap, a sterile jet casts down
Thin remnants, still organic, and disbands
Properties and substances. Gone
Are titles and inheritances, lost
All strict distinctions, measurements, the rites
Established and the uttered words, the crossed
Accoutrements of faith, extinguished lights
Under a length of earth, a breadth of days,
Changed elements of change.

            My knuckles rough
From picking at those seams, my skin learns ways
Of covering up, of healing, and grows tough.

ELEGY

Something of the earth it has, something of dust:
It has a solid feel, and yet it drifts
With sudden tugs of breeze
Into new shape, new movement. The wind lifts
And brings the weaker branches to their knees.
Something shifts down to earth because it must.

Let it lie there, silent and full of years:
It will still move within its chosen space,
Its patterned diagram
Laid out before it, staring in the face
Something it is, and something I too am
Beyond the elegy, beyond the tears.

RISING

And here it is, washed up, dumped, spread
Along the tideless shore, the spoil
Of centuries, the abandoned dead,
The looted remnants torn and ditched,
Smoke rising from the fired hotel,
And over all a heavy smell,
An arm surrendering, outstretched
To ask for mercy, and a cry
Of hopelessness, or victory.

So back and forth the rumours run
Of triumph, of annihilation.
Fragments of rage rise up and echo
While scattered men race to and fro
Proclaiming who has lost or won.

WAITING IN

They promised to deliver. So I wait
All day, and listen for the bell. The hours
Go by from morning until noon, and late
Into the afternoon. Nothing arrives.
The time drifts off in bits like vanished lives.
The windows show dark clouds like distant towers.

A bruised June sky. My birthday came and went.
Now I wait in, have nothing else to do
Except to wait and let the time be spent
In counting minutes, restless, fidgeting,
Unable to get on with anything,
Watching the traffic down the avenue.

Now it's too late. Nothing will come today.
A waste of time, a whole day gone like this,
Emptily, with such trivial delay
Nagging at age and irritation. When
I draw the heavy curtains, restless, then
The waiting-in slips into sleeplessness

And a whole day of waiting starts again.

ON THARSTON BRIDGE

Water under the bridge – dead metaphor
Lifted from somewhere, left to lie
Stiff on the page. Yet now it comes to life
Simply by being written down, repeated
Like something in the liturgy, words chanted
And echoing down the old cold labyrinths.
I pick them up and warm them on my tongue
Bringing back all that happened long ago
And flowed away, yet also can be seen
Far down under the parapets, going on,
Not to be stopped or hindered, staying there
In bits and pieces, shatterings and sherds,
Not to be joined together and made whole
But water under the bridge, still flowing on.

MOON AGAIN

And still up there, polluted, trodden down,
Your dust scuffed up, your hollows mapped and clear,
You watch us still but vaguely, out of touch,
Reached yet irrelevant, your glow diminished
Because familiar, stained with rhetoric,
Like some old politician one thought dead.

Now exploration reaches past your gaze,
Is insolent with yearnings far beyond,
Ticking off swirling bodies one by one.
Your distance, beauty, mystery are betrayed,
Your sweet enigma fades away and dies,
And red-eyed Mars swarms with new buccaneers.

WORDS OF COMFORT FROM A BED OF PAIN

Trigeminal neuralgia, sciatica –
These great Romano-Graecisms, disabling, dominate:
Not 'life-threatening' but telling me each day
Each day is closer to the end of things.
At first I scream, take handfuls of bright pills,
Then settle down to hobbling here and there
Governed by gentle repetition, little ploys –
Of how to dress myself, sit up, sit down,
Move across rooms, at last flop into bed.
It's like a parody of infancy
But now fixed at the far end of my life,
A kind of preparation. Well, I'm cheered
By habit, little victories, another day
Pushing the pain a few minutes away,
Locked in an ungovernable spasm.
Exercise is no good: I've read the books
And peered at diagrams, and tried the lot,
Then, lashed into some fixed-tight Gordian knot
And my right jaw shot with electric shock,
I wait till the things die down, and brood on death
Which cannot be like this, must be far off,
A something which is nothing, not these medical
Theatrical mouthings of Graeco-Roman vocables.

CREDO

Yes, I believe, but what do I believe?
Leave out the bits conveniently that stick
Stiff in my throat and seem much too absurd,
Or look too much a conjuror's bad trick,
All those measurements of Arks (Noah's and Covenant's)
As if they mattered, Paul laying down the law unyieldingly,
Or churches filled with soft moans and cheery ditties
Like some third-rate American musical,
Waugh's 'chapter of blood-curdling military history',
And bleating synods bickering over women...

The objections are so many, the stumbling-blocks
Trip me at almost every turn, until
Exhaustion makes me silent. Dare I say:
Yes, I believe, because despite all that
It's true and trusted, and I hear him speak
Clear in his mysteries direct to me?
The accusers come to demand his rough judgement.
He scratches something in the dust, and finds
The woman taken in adultery standing there
Alone, and the accusers crept away
Knowing their guilt, knowing their impotence.

The gentle riddles of the parables,
That last great cry high on the bloody cross,
The stone rolled back, and Mary suddenly
Knowing his voice, and all the voices raised
At Pentecost in those alien tongues,
Appearing, disappearing, going on,
The bread and wine, the simple reached-for things
So difficult to swallow. Yet I believe.
'Lord, I believe: help thou my unbelief'.

PROLOGUE TO AN UNFINISHED POSTHUMOUS POEM

> While every day my hairs fall more and more,
> My hand shakes, and the heavy years increase –
>
> Browning, *Cleon*

I am beginning now a late work,
Possibly my last, as I sit here in my pain
Trying to prod the fire into action.
What I have in mind, among other things,
Is an accurate catalogue of my contemporaries,
Sparing nothing, as a record of these times
When fatuous reputations far and wide
Are made by hard careerists and soft triflers.

The metaphor that comes to mind is 'rubbish':
They move it round from place to place each day
Shifting the smashed discarded worthless waste,
Crumpled and dusty, bits that thrown away
Crumble, turn to mush, disintegrate.
The basket overflows its bulging wires
Distended with its crap crammed down, a task
Too big for fifty sweepers and their brooms.

Or consider the forensic theory of interchange:
'It is impossible to enter or leave
A situation without leaving something behind
Or taking something away.' What will be left of these
Diurnal charlatans who leave behind a trail
Of paper droppings, like stuff gnawed by mice?
They fill the journals with their whimsies, or they glower
Stiff with their bleak tight-lipped grim rectitudes.

Well, I suppose I must now begin
To launch into this enterprise with speed
Before the reaper stretches out his blade
And takes me off without another word.
Another metaphor, another phrase
Caught in my throat. The stuff lies here so thick –
But I must try to clear the ground, and start
This record of the rubbish all around…

AND WHERE

And where we go from here no one can say:
Whether far away
Or round the corner, hidden,
Perhaps sudden
Coming down like a blind,
And whatever lies behind
As dark as midnight, or as bright as day.

And will we recognise the place when we get there,
A familiar air
Smelling like fields we knew,
And see the true
Path we must follow now,
No matter how
We wondered when we landed here; or where?

OUT OF TUNE

These are uneasy promptings, vague as air,
Wandering without shape
Through music's measurements, down the steep slope
That leads nowhere.

The footsteps of the music miss a beat,
Stumble, perhaps, or fall
Silently, till a cry heard from the street
Restores it all.

CREATION MYTH

The version that says 'Six Days' is still up for grabs
In certain Southern states; though the Big Bang's
More popular along seashores where the crabs
Seem to be mutating, and life hangs

In the balance. Where do you stand, or fall, or rise
On this long-debated question? It's absurd
To ask it, maybe, when most mysteries
Are swept under the carpet, and the Word

Is seldom spoken without silent doubt.
As if it might go away with no trouble,
A huge amnesiac door marked IN and OUT
Turns on its hinges through the crushed rubble.

God as Moloch, or the great inventor,
Presides over Creation, the Fall, the Coming Again,
As you press the button, the button that says 'Enter'.
Nothing that happens ever happens in vain.

i. m. PETER READING, 1946–2011

Despair; desuetude; drink –
Not a bad trio
To celebrate in concert

One who hammered out music
Percussive, classic,
Whatever's left of something

Plangent, bereft, and bankrupt:
The dying planet
Drifting down to daft giggles.

TO PETER PORTER IN BALMAIN, N.S.W., FROM ANTHONY THWAITE IN CARDOSO, PROVINZIA DI LUCCA, TUSCANY

Dear Peter, while on leave from Melvin Lasky,
And having put down one or two *fiasci*
Of *vino rosso dolce e locale*,
I write to you above this happy valley
Some thirty miles or so due north of Lucca.
I've read your new anthology (a book a
Bigot might call a thoroughgoing *cento*
Of all in English verse that's cashed and spent – O
Where is 'the roll, the rise, the carol, the creation'?)
Enough of that. Today it's with elation
I sit down to commemorate for you
The local scene laid out, an overview
Of part of Italy we never saw
When you and I were travelling here before:
Unmapped by Porter/Thwaite, unsnapped by Beny,
But certainly as beautiful as any.
Ron and Marie, our friends, have bought a *casa*
Built at one end of this small town's *piazza*.
A century ago, the chestnut tree:
Dictated the whole town's economy
They burnt it, ate it, built with it, made paper
Out of its pulp; but Time, that grim old raper,
Has changed all that. The northerners descended
After the reign of *Re Castagno* ended,
And bought the shells of Tuscan houses through
Agents who made them twice as good as new.
Not that the whole place has been dispossessed:
The villagers inhabit all the rest,
Accepting the incomers apparently
With half amusement and half courtesy.
Across the valley, where a climbing car is
Ascending one-in-eight, lives A. Alvarez,

Or so I'm told: I haven't seen him yet.
The other side there dwells 'the denim set'
(So christened by my daughters) – North-West-Three
Adepts of lucrative psychiatry,
A Kleinian husband and a Kleinian wife,
Which seems to me a recipe for strife
(To me – to you, I guess – who follows Melanie
Is guilty of a double compound felony),
But Dr Shrink has somehow played it cool,
If one can judge from his vast swimming-pool.
He plied us all with home-made *sangria*
While conversation turned on R. D. Laing: we are
Approved of by their teenage sons, who took a shine
To Lucy, Emily and Caroline –
Pale daughters of the north who blossom here
Where sun and wine have vanquished rain and beer
(Not that the other stuff is rare, of course,
Though ice-cold tubes of Foster's nipped at source:
'The denim set' drives up the hill to Barga
To set about the crates of local lager).
Rocks poise precariously: *caduta massi*
Lie all around to stun the teen-age lassy,
Unless she's fallen already for young Tino,
Giuseppe, Roberto, Alberto, Rocco, Gino
Or other youths along the *Garfagnana*
Who fancy northern flesh's white arcana.
Cardoso has a Chelsea decorator
But what I know of him must wait till later –
Another epic, at least another canto
Written from the Castle of Otranto.
It has an Englishman who teaches art
To rich Americans in Florence (part
Of coals-to-Newcastle, you may well think,
Though really not much odder than Doc Shrink,
But drawing-masters based on old Firenze

Can drive the local matrons to a frenzy).
A weapons-man on leave from ITT
Has temporarily left his weaponry:
A hundred thousand dollars are shelled out
To turn his roofs and terraces all about –
Floor becomes ceiling, wash-house gleaming loo,
The builders' feigning art becomes the true,
A modest house transformed to Xanadu.
The only snag – a scorpion on the wall
Balefully winks at Belshazzar Q. Baal.

The natives are too various to mention,
But I'll just offer one for your attention –
A follower of a far from silent Order,
The priest employs a faulty tape-recorder,
With bells that peal out through an amplifier,
A vile perversion of the heavenly choir.

But this epistolary lucubration
Has moved too far from simple celebration.
Let me give praise, let me unloose an ode
Along wide *autostrada* or dirt road.
Bergamo, Verona, Venice, Lucca,
Siena, Florence, Pisa – yes, we took a
Look at the peninsula on the wing,
And all agreed there isn't anything
Quite like it anywhere. Land of the *mezzo-
Litro*, from Carrara to Arezzo,
From Val D'Aosta to far Siracusa,
There's nowhere nicer for the *vino*-boozer,
The ruin-bibber, the snoozer in the sun,
In fact the ideal place for everyone.
Byron and Shelley, Landor and Ouida,
Took Tuscan bases for the English reader –
And for a fortnight, so do I for you,

Though now I fear my letter's almost through:
We belt through chunks of Alp, Montreux, Lausanne,
Through miserable France in groaning van,
And up to Belgium (nasty, brutish, short)
And – just in time – have North Sea Ferry caught
(Excuse the shorthand – scribbling in this way
Seems to have knocked my metre all agley).
The rain comes down, the northern breezes blow,
The ferry wafts us back to Felixstowe;
And so farewell to golden Italy –
Arrivederci, Peter, to you from me.

August 1975

RUNES FOR PETER

Ten years ago, I mobilised your friends
(Or twenty of them) to celebrate in prose
Or verse your three-score years and ten;*
And now that decad (no final 'e') ends,
Which only shows
The difference between the 'now' and 'then'
Comes down to figures, meaningless and pale.
My earliest school report was plain; it said
'Anthony has no sense of number'. True –
My numbering of the passing years grows stale:
Instead,
Let my 'no sense of number' see us through.

* *Paeans for Peter Porter*, Bridgewater Press, 1999

VITA SOMNIUM BREVE (PT. 2)

(for Peter Porter)

And I too remember Veronica,
That tremendously English moniker,
With her violet eyes,
Her Empsonian disguise,
And her air that she'd just drunk a tonic a'
nd gin to begin
A life full of sin,
Except that the whole air of cleverness
Rejected all sex and togetherness.

I think you were taken
With her life stirred and shaken
By some French *philosophe*
With tubercular cough,
That life on the edge
Had driven a wedge
Into Cambridge and Barthes and *Tel Quel*
And had left her living in Hell
And the Avant-Garde went on
And on and on and on,
Without dignity, purpose, or sense,
Leaving her in the past tense,
Till your poem in *Better Than God*
Which, I think you'll admit
(Australian 'No shit'),
Is a little bit odd.

FOR PETER PORTER

'A troubled Deist' – so you said,
With that shrugged grin and tilted head,
Sharp self-defining. Now you're dead,
  Those words come back.
You lay exhausted on the bed.
  On the soundtrack

Some stuff you called 'just music', not
Your masters Bach and Mozart, what
The thing pumped out – not utter rot
  Yet not front-rank.
Meanwhile, your room was stifling hot,
  Your body shrank

Down to its elements, ready to go,
And we all tiptoed to and fro,
Your breathing heavy, painful, slow.
  Last week, you said
'You find me in dire straits', as though
  Poised to be dead.

Yet with a firm contemptuous snort
You'd told me when I'd asked what sort
Of sending-off you maybe thought
  Would be the best –
'No *humanist* funeral'. In short,
  To lay at rest

In plain old-fashioned Anglican
Ritual the mortal man
Was your considered final plan,
  And now it's done.
The reading's stopped, the lines all scan,
  The race is run.

A WORD OF ADVICE

(*for Peter Scupham at 70*)

Shun the strewn bone-grounds, cemeteries and barrows,
Keep out of churchyards, and avoid the grave:
That ploughshare has pursued too many furrows,
It knows too well how death-bed bards behave.

An elegiac stance is always easy,
A flask of tears is always close to hand:
If all else fails, and taste is turning queasy,
A lamentation's what they understand

Who have some taste for verse, and rhyme, and metre,
Who think a poem is a Grecian Urn,
Who find an elegy is somehow sweeter
Than reckoning up what unearned sorrows earn.

So, Peter, my advice you've often quoted
Is partly serious, though said in jest:
However the majority has voted,
Staying alive is always for the best.

SKELTONICS FOR HUGO WILLIAMS
AT SEVENTY

What a profile!
Meanwhile
Death carried on its way,
Week by week, day by day,
Lopping off Donaghy,
Imlah, old Bertie,
Narrowing down to this
Denizen of Is-
lington, still going on
Reaping its glum way,
Until today
Confronted by this man
Age cannot wither,
It says 'Why bother?'
And gives up while it can.

THE LIFE AND DEATH OF THE PINE PROCESSIONARY

Soundtrack for a BBC documentary film

This is a garden for the cultivation of death.
Here under glass the leaves and pine-branches have only
    one purpose:
to harbour sickness, to carry disease, to destroy –
and *I* have been marked down.
The name they give me is the Pine Processionary, and I
    am legion.

In the pine forests of Provence I live in my thick and
    tangled colonies
for a little while longer.

In Spring, my colonies wake one day
to discover a place where I must change in some way.
What I am looking for
is powdery soil or sand, granules in the sun,
where I must bury myself. In procession
I spin a silken thread, each to each,
to mark a clear path for my slow progress,
my metamorphosis.

But some must fall by the way, for we have enemies:
the hot acids of the ant, sharper than his sharp beak,
spill into me and madden me. From my clefts and segments
I volley out my lances, my brittle hairs,
in a fine poisonous dust. Some must fall, ants and caterpillars.
My tough survivors start out again, and then
huddle together, ready for another kind of burial.

Each weaves his shroud, shutting out the light,
mimicking death, a phoenix bedded down
in sand and silk, not fire.

I am beginning to be born again,
my head a steel-hard drill, tunnelling upwards,
scattering sand-grains and pebbles, flailing the earth aside,
ponderous, blind, earthbound,
a brown lump of damp tissue,
heaving myself over the punishing earth.

But the air is my nurse, and the sun. They draw
my wings into life, I stretch, I rise up, I move
tentative, painful, suddenly aware
of constriction moving away, of a new power
which is not wholly mine, my whole purpose in life to propagate
and, that done, to die again:

the brief clumsy act, and then our separate deaths –
the male, shaken and feeble, utterly spent;
the female, a little while longer to lay her eggs,
then also twitching, dying.

Even those eggs, packed tight among the pine needles,
are vulnerable. The cricket is hungry for them.

Gulped in succulent mandibles,
the prodigal waste of life is measured out.
But enough survive. After a month, those of us left
hatch out into a world of air and food.

Spin and pirouette,
peer and bob and nod and toddle,
walk the high tightrope of the silk thread,
dance, for a while, dance.

After the fiery ant and the predatory cricket,
the obscene lunging fly, choked and brimming
with a sluiceful of white eggs, choosing our youngest
as compost for her own young, who will feed
through the tunnels of our bodies, leaving some
mere husks, the dead receptacles of the living,
hosts for parasites.

But again, my will is to survive:
enough of us to spin our white cities
safe against all enemies we know,
or have known until now.

These are our forests, empires of sustenance,
ripe for our feasting, the delicate shoots of pine
laid out in liberal acres, a whole emporium
ripe for our gluttony.

The sweetness of this food, soft and hard!
Eat, eat,
till our cities bulge with our full bodies,
the trees where we munch great banquets of the night,
a steady roar of appetite, of greed.

At dawn, bloated, we lace and loop ourselves
back to our cities, finding our gorged way
with threads spun in the evening in the trees.

And when the Spring returns
the other trees, the trees we do not know,
put on their buds and leaves and live again.
But the pines have been consumed, are in our bellies.

Now, after the ravages of the ant,
the cricket and the fly,
time for a new and deadlier enemy: man.
Man, to protect his forests, builds a forest
under roofs, under glass, among white and sterile things
that never knew life at all:
an abattoir for insects.

My diseased body, its guts swollen with the one
virus wholly my own:
the long incision lays it bare, to let leak out
my innermost enemy, a milky stuff
crammed with my own death, to be multiplied,
a virus…
        a virus isolated, magnified,
a many-sided weapon, sharp-edged, focused
on my annihilation,
to be crushed into liquid, agitated, then
rendered to fragments, fed to me at last –
so that I eat my death and breed it too.

Five weeks, and the virus has destroyed all those
fed from the poisoned twigs, and yet no other creature
will die because of this. Mild to all other creatures,
to us it spells out death.

So from the slopes of Mont Ventoux, the slopes
which our great cities colonised and scoured,
men gather a miniature forest of death, and feed
half a million of us, the healthy ones –
picked for our health, but picked to kill the rest.
Each nest we build, each colony, shuts in
two hundred caterpillars, all condemned.

Where once we danced, we hang – a parody
of all our dancing youthful ancestors.
The dead are counted,
a monotonous declension, a catalogue of deaths.

From flesh to liquid to dust, a lethal powder mixed
to put an end to all of us: a mere
forty tons, they say, to exterminate
the greedy armies, the eaters of the pines.

Over the hills,
over the pine forests, the great bird flies
over and over, poisoning us alone.

The epidemic spreads, the corpses hang
dustily in the trees, to be swept away
by the Spring winds, turned to dust, made dust
by dust from our own bodies.

Over the hills,
over the pine forests, the great bird flies
over and over, poisoning us alone
as the dust swirls and falls in its long, deliberate skeins.

The procession halts. The processionary dies.
The hills remain, and the forests, and the men.

JUBILEE LINES

The day the King died I was telling Pryce
To pull his socks up or he'd never get
His Common Entrance. Heronwater School
('Ten acres of Welsh parkland, healthy air,
The boys encouraged to be self-reliant')
Employed me as a temporary beak,
Poised for two terms between demob and that
Long-dreamt-of unimaginable life
Which Oxford promised. Heronwater taught
The pre-pubertal boys of prosperous
Yorkshire and Lancashire to pass with ease
To Oundle, Repton, Rugby, Uppingham,
With one or two to Harrow, and a few
(Almost unmentionable) who, lacking funds,
Vanished to grammar schools. I taught them bits
Of English, History, Geography, coached teams
In rugger and athletics, took the Scouts
Out in the woods for nature trails and how
To tie a clove-hitch, half-hitch, reef and splice,
Supervised 'Numbers' (euphemistic term
For bodily evacuations, front
And back, kept carefully for the Matron's eye),
Had carnal knowledge of the Music mistress
(A woman built on megalithic lines),
Went drinking in Welsh-speaking pubs with Bill
(The Classics master and an unfrocked priest),
Discovered R. S. Thomas, whose whole work
In two slim pamphlets printed locally
I bought in Hughes the Stationers in Rhyl,
And wrote verse letters to my army friend,
Brian, a communist in Chingford. This
Was 1952, when ration-books
Were still required for sweets, when girls wore sheer

Nylons with difficult suspenders, and
Malaya and Korea took our troops
And turned them into corpses. Twenty-one,
Gloomy, ambitious, callow, veteran
Graduate of the Educational Corps,
Messing about with poetry and sex,
Getting nowhere with either, did I care
When Smythe, the Second Master, knocked and came
Into the class where I was chiding Pryce,
And said, 'The King is dead'? I can't remember,
But hear the Dead March out of Handel's *Saul*
The BBC played hour after hour
That day, and probably the next day too.
Classes were cancelled, I suppose, the Head
Held an assembly in the hall that served
As part-time chapel, where his favourite lesson
Was Sisera and the tent-peg. If I'd known
That quarter of a century afterwards
I'd be invited by a Festival
To write a poem for the Jubilee
Of the King's daughter, how would I have felt?
Impossible to say. The things that happen
And go on happening are a vaporous whirl
Of incidents and nothings, a vague flux
Soon to be memories or else forgotten,
Whether a nation's history or the sum
Total we think of as a human life,
A decade or a century, a reign,
A period, an epoch, or a day.
To catalogue the years between, to scan
My life or England's, to produce a hymn
Appropriate as hymns must always be –
Beyond my powers. I stand here, middle-aged,
Looking on lands I own, with children, wife,
Accumulations, publications, years
Of busyness and idleness and swarms

Of pleasures and regrets and this and that,
Alive, half-kicking when I want to kick
Which isn't often, puzzled sometimes, more
Lost in a way than that unlined young sprig
Who told off Pryce for slacking on the day
The King died, and the Dead March out of *Saul*
Thundered across the Home and Light and Third.
Dear Honorary Organiser, this
May 'have some relevance to the twenty-five
Years of the Queen's reign,' reflect 'changing patterns',
As your kind letter back in February
Suggested. That the GLC will choose
To carve these sentences 'in slate or stone
To be sited on the South Bank' I must doubt.
No disrespect for monarchy or indeed
Ilkley intended; at another time,
Say back in '87 or '97,
Ancestral voices might have brought it off,
In pious quatrains, stanzas rich and ripe,
Confident odes, psalmodic harmonies.
But not today. The reasons why must wait
For those historians – if such exist –
A hundred years or so from now,
Strange creatures unforeseeable by us,
Peering at yellowing archives, holding up
For scrutiny our foibles and our fears,
These oddities; and one of them may find
These rambling, ambling lines, and spend all day
Writing a footnote to establish who
The schoolboy Pryce was, mentioned by one 'Thwaite',
Active in the first quarter-century
Of Queen Elizabeth the Second, now
Forgotten totally, equally obscure
In Ilkley, Nova Zembla, Samarkand,
A small voice lost among the drifted years.

SIX SENILE SENRYU

D. H. Lawrence dead
And Auden's *Poems* published –
In between, my birth.

Pop, fizz – not champagne
Let off in celebration:
False teeth in that glass.

Climbing this ladder,
A sudden dizzy tremor –
Earthquake, body-quake?

The name I search for
Familiar as the back of –
Isn't that my hand?

Four times a night, now,
Getting up to have a pee,
Steady as heartbeats.

Try to remember
The poem you invented…
How does it begin?

Appalling plunderings of sense and sound,
A music insidious and profound
But meaningless in any paraphrase:
It deafened and seduced me in those days
When echoes echoed everywhere, and words
Clustered in congregations like bright birds.
Absurd and wonderful and long ago,
Too far now out of sight for me to know
Whether they were illusion, vision, or
A truth I had not ever known before
And have lost since. They echo out of range,
Blurred syllables of youth, of noise, of change.

REVISITED

(a memory of my mother)

The Terrace, Vyner Street, and Portland House,
Edinburgh Terrace, Grosvenor Terrace, Lindsay Street –
We track these childhood lodgings, and turn here
To Shipton Elementary, and on
To Walmgate and the slums of Bootham Row.

Eighty years past, and you remember them,
Name them, and tell me now it's second left
To Markham Crescent: fly-by-night flits, a pall
That's not yet lifted from that shameful past,
Dodging the rent, your father skipped again.

Out on the city's edge, the pleasant places –
Easingwold, Coxwold, Skelton, Crayke, where you
Sometimes forgot the bailiffs, pawnshop, splits
That sent you to a sister, cousin, friend.
But each name is remembered as we go

Back for the first time in decrepitude
Through lanes and ginnels, through each charter'd street,
To find a past I see you now inherit,
Brave in old age to shrug it off, content
To hand it on to me, be free of it.

INSCRUTABLE

(a memory of China, 1980)

Emerging with gallery feet
From the Beijing Museum
(All later than Sung shut off
'For one month's repairs'),
I walked through the empty square
(Parade ground; no parade),
Sat on the steps of the Monument
To the Peoples' Heroes, lit a fag,

Read the guidebook – and looked up
To find four soldiers watching
At a polite distance.
Then old and young came by,
Dragging reluctant children,
Clutching a baby or two.
They stopped, and began to stare.
More soldiers, more granddads, until

Forty or so stood there,
In a circle around the steps
Where I sat like a statue on show.
'I am English', I said, in English:
'I am a friend', I said.
They stared as I blushed and shrugged,
And watched as I stood and walked
Out of the square, alone.

THE COLOURS OF LONDON
(after Yoshio Markino, 1911)

Colours of women, a grey-veiled pink, a bloom
Fading to yellow, stippled, dust-hung, flecked
Soot startling white lace in summer gloom.

Colours of trees, pavements sticky with leaves
Trodden to blackened bronze, a patina
Attached to every twig. The heart grieves,

Colours the blood with fungus, smudges all
Spires, bridges, waters, with its spores,
Catches each raindrop as the bruised clouds fall.

Colours – the names of them, the languages
Seeping between – slip into sepia,
Then steely white, as words freeze images.

Colours of women, trees, blood, stone on stone
Piled high, dismantled, crowded as a dream
Night after night in London, and alone.

STRING QUARTET, NEW BUCKENHAM CASTLE

These four frail instruments confront the ruined world
And all that is not ruined. Rooks, doves, gulls
Drift, float and fall above the pleated air,
The blue of June, the sound of air distilled:
Each chord extends, then gathers, captures, pulls
Our scattered selves into a theatre,
Something made separate now made together.
So, stitched and disparate, the music fills
The castle's crumbled stone, the slumped distracted ear,
Chatter of children, distant engine roar,
The past's still ruin, the present's decibels,
Hovering above, descending gently here
Decisively, precisely, till it stills
To silence that is nowhere, everywhere.

SIGNS

Unambiguous signs: crossed twigs on pavements,
Leaves pointing a certain way, words through the wall
Dictated by Dr Ernst – these are all
Clear indications of what is going on,
All adding up to truth, all making sense
Until all sense without patterning has gone.

When there is nothing else a single bulb
Burns in the brain all night, all day, to light
The certain darkness. The uncertain self
Searches for what it is certain must be right.

Out in the street the wind blows all one way
To point the trees where they and you must go.
Their lifted leaves all mutter to and fro.

Now there is neither light nor night nor day.

QUESTIONS

Shall I begin with the papers on my desk,
The papers on my bed, the papers on the floor,
Or the books tilting over on the very top shelf,
Or the books on the stairs, or the books on my desk,
Or shall I get on with the antiquarian scraps
Silting up on the sill, or in boxes on the floor,
Or the cabinet-drawers, or behind the cupboard door,
Or still to be found in cupboards I've forgotten,
Or stuffed into corners of the shed or the barn,
Or elbowed into somewhere altogether elsewhere,
Or piles piled up in pillars of papers
Unsteady in my head as I try to begin to
Sort the papers on the desk, on the bed, on the floor,
And shift them a little and open the door?

THE SEVENTH AGE

Envy, the sour sister I never had:
Anger, my fitful brother never known –
They come now, late in age, and make me sad,
Familiar siblings who left me on my own.

The others I once knew have dropped away:
Lust, greed, and sloth – I recognise them all
But know them no longer. If they meant to stay
They never told me; and they never call.

A little covetous, a little proud –
These I admit, but as an only child
Had little need to hide them. When allowed
I hoarded coins; was priggish, and not wild.

So I am left with only these close kin
In my imagination, hard to face:
Envy at those who effortlessly win,
Anger at losing, lacking that good grace.

IN THE VICINITY OF THE CRANK-HOUSE

I am becoming a connoisseur of walking sticks,
Comparing my own stout stump with the slender ferrule,
The harsh metal wand, or the pair of hospital crutches.

Not lameness or amputation, thank God, simply old age
And a condition known as 'degenerative spine' –
Something between a moral menace and a washed-out weakling.

In the vicinity of the crank-house the maimed swing by
As I make my own slow way between sets of traffic lights,
Grinning a greeting grimly in complicitous courtesy.

My first was something much lighter, with a silver band,
But I had to leave that behind as my back shrank.
Sometimes I journey uphill muttering to myself

That bit of Christina Rossetti in a stertorous way.
There are worse ways of being a connoisseur
Than quoting Christina Rossetti, and comparing walking-sticks.

FERNANDO LOBO

My dark Brazilian friend, seventy years back
In Washington. Both of us were foreign,
On the edge of Gordon Junior High.
After my English prep-school shine wore off,
My grades slid down and I lost interest
In most things, except stamps and snakes and sex.
We visited the embassies, cadging stamps,
And messed about off Massachusetts Avenue
Playing the hub-cap trick on passing cars
(You threw one into the road and shouted "Hub-cap!"
And the car screeched to a halt.)
                            All this was idle,
The sort of stuff thirteen-year-olds get up to.
But you, somehow, made it all different,
A different way of foreign-ness, a mask
To wear until a real face appeared,
And I went home to England, and the war
Ended, and I forgot Fernando Lobo
Until last night I dreamt of your dark smile,
Conspiratorial, and foreign, just like me.

THE LINE

The line came out of nowhere as I woke.
I rose and wrote it down.
                              And then I lost it,
And ever since have rummaged everywhere
Trying to find those few good words I'd found
Without knowing I'd found them.
                              Walking at night
Or waking at dawn, my mind is busy
Fretting to find again those lost few words:
They had authority, and a fine tune as well,
Together in one line that would lead on
To others just as fine, a solid shape
Not to be shifted.
                              But all of it has gone
Into a nowhere that I cannot reach,
Drifted away, out on the furthest edge.

CLASSICAL TEXT

Rub out the colours of imagination
And cut the puppet's strings.
Do not anticipate a higher station.
Only birds have wings.

See things for what they are: the choked ditch,
Dulled sodden grass, the sun
Leaning against the sky. Know which is which,
Carrion, skeleton.

Inhabit your cube of air easily.
Confine your care to what
Presents itself as now, and presently
Withdraw from the lot.

Rub out the colours of imagination,
See what there is to see.
Thus the imperial meditation,
180 A.D.

TIME TO GO

Feeling my age, too soon too tired,
Whatever gifts I had no more required,
I am a hireling called in to be fired.
Time was I was ambitious, heretofore.
Not any more, not any more.

Ridding myself of papers, pots, coins, books,
No longer vain about what had been looks,
The broth boiled over by too many cooks.
Time was I kept some goods held back in store.
Not any more, not any more.

Taking my time over this last short walk,
Not hearing what I say, or how I talk,
Pushing my knife against my trembling fork.
Time was I knew when I'd become a bore.
Not any more, not any more.

ACKNOWLEDGEMENTS AND NOTES

Several of these poems first appeared in the following: *London Review of Books, Poetry Review, Spectator, Standpoint, The Shop, The Times Literary Supplement, Warwick Review*.

A few were prompted by 'occasions', others by actual commissions. I give some details:

'To Peter Porter in Balmain, N.S.W. ...' was written in 1975 as a letter when Peter was on a long stay in Australia and I was on holiday in Italy; it appeared eventually in *Paeans for Peter Porter* in 1999, but not elsewhere.

'Runes for Peter' was written for his eightieth birthday in 2009 and, as the poem indicates, follows the book I edited secretly for his seventieth, *Paeans for Peter Porter* (Bridgewater Press, 1999).

'Vita Somnium Breve (pt. 2)' followed a poem written by Porter with the title 'Vita Somnium Breve' in memory of the poet Veronica Forrest-Thomson (1947–1975).

'For Peter Porter' was written soon after his death in April 2010.

Both 'A Word of Advice (for Peter Scupham at 70)' and 'Skeltonics for Hugo Williams' were the result of private commissions and have not previously been published.

'The Life and Death of the Pine Processionary' was the result of a commission by BBC 2 television for the 'Horizon' series. It was first published in *Inscriptions* (OUP, 1973) but not in a collected volume.

'Jubilee Lines' was the result of a commission by the Ilkley Literature Festival celebrating the Queen's Silver Jubilee. It was read at the Festival, broadcast by the BBC, and printed in a large format publication with the title *Happy and Glorious* (Scolar Press, 1977), along with poems by sundry other poets (including Fleur Adcock, Patricia Beer, Charles Causley, Gavin Ewart, Roy Fuller and Charles Tomlinson) but never published elsewhere.